EMMANUEL JOSEPH

The Transnational Brand Equation, Crafting Irresistible Global Marketing Strategies

Copyright © 2025 by Emmanuel Joseph

All rights reserved. No part of this publication may be reproduced, stored or transmitted in any form or by any means, electronic, mechanical, photocopying, recording, scanning, or otherwise without written permission from the publisher. It is illegal to copy this book, post it to a website, or distribute it by any other means without permission.

First edition

*This book was professionally typeset on Reedsy.
Find out more at reedsy.com*

Contents

1. Chapter 1: Understanding the Transnational Market — 1
2. Chapter 2: Building a Strong Brand Identity — 3
3. Chapter 3: Market Research and Consumer Insights — 5
4. Chapter 4: Crafting a Compelling Brand Story — 7
5. Chapter 5: Leveraging Digital Marketing Channels — 9
6. Chapter 6: The Role of Influencer Marketing — 11
7. Chapter 7: Navigating Legal and Regulatory Challenges — 13
8. Chapter 8: Effective Cross-Cultural Communication — 15
9. Chapter 9: Localizing Your Marketing Campaigns — 17
10. Chapter 10: Building Strong Partnerships — 19
11. Chapter 11: Measuring Success and ROI — 21
12. Chapter 12: Adapting to Changing Market Trends — 23
13. Chapter 13: Embracing Sustainability and Social... — 25
14. Chapter 14: Navigating Crises and Challenges — 27
15. Chapter 15: The Future of Transnational Marketing — 29

1

Chapter 1: Understanding the Transnational Market

In today's interconnected world, the marketplace has transcended geographical boundaries, transforming local businesses into global entities. To succeed in this expansive arena, companies must grasp the complexities of transnational markets, where consumer behaviors, preferences, and cultural nuances vary significantly. The global marketplace is no longer a distant concept; it is the reality that businesses operate within, and understanding it is the first step toward crafting irresistible global marketing strategies.

One of the fundamental principles of transnational marketing is cultural sensitivity. Successful brands recognize that a one-size-fits-all approach does not work in diverse markets. Instead, they adopt a transnational mindset, which involves understanding and respecting the cultural differences that influence consumer behavior. This mindset allows brands to tailor their products, messaging, and marketing campaigns to resonate with local audiences while maintaining a consistent global identity.

The importance of cultural intelligence cannot be overstated. It is the ability to navigate and adapt to different cultural contexts effectively. Brands that invest in cultural intelligence are better equipped to understand their target markets, anticipate consumer needs, and build strong, lasting relationships. This chapter delves into real-world examples of brands that have successfully embraced cultural intelligence and the lessons they offer for aspiring transnational marketers.

Globalization has played a pivotal role in shaping the transnational market. It has created a web of interconnected economies, where local events can have global repercussions. For brands, this means staying informed about global trends and being agile enough to adapt to changing market conditions. By examining the impact of globalization on consumer behavior and market dynamics, this chapter provides a comprehensive understanding of the transnational market landscape.

That's a start! Now, let's continue with Chapter 2.

2

Chapter 2: Building a Strong Brand Identity

A compelling brand identity is the cornerstone of any successful marketing strategy, especially in a transnational context. It serves as the foundation upon which all marketing efforts are built. However, in a global marketplace, a brand identity must be flexible enough to resonate with diverse audiences while maintaining a consistent core message. Striking this balance is key to building a strong, recognizable brand that can thrive in different cultural contexts.

The elements of brand identity, such as logo design, messaging, and brand values, play a crucial role in shaping how a brand is perceived. In a transnational setting, these elements must be carefully crafted to ensure they are culturally relevant and appealing. This chapter explores the process of creating a brand identity that stands out in the global marketplace, with a focus on adaptability and cultural sensitivity.

Real-world examples of successful transnational brands provide valuable insights into effective brand identity strategies. These case studies highlight how brands have navigated cultural differences, adapted their messaging, and maintained consistency across diverse markets. By learning from these examples, readers will gain practical knowledge on how to build a brand identity that resonates with global audiences.

In addition to the visual and messaging aspects of brand identity, brand values play a significant role in shaping consumer perceptions. In a transnational context, these values must align with the cultural norms and expectations of different markets. Brands that successfully integrate their values into their identity can build stronger connections with consumers and foster loyalty. This chapter delves into the importance of brand values and how they can be communicated effectively in a global marketplace.

3

Chapter 3: Market Research and Consumer Insights

In the vast and diverse global marketplace, understanding your target audience is paramount. Effective market research is the key to unlocking valuable consumer insights that can guide your marketing strategies. This chapter delves into the importance of market research in a transnational context and explores various methods for gathering and analyzing data across different regions.

To craft marketing strategies that resonate with diverse audiences, brands must first understand the unique characteristics of each market. This involves conducting thorough market research to gather data on consumer behaviors, preferences, and cultural nuances. By leveraging tools such as surveys, focus groups, and social media analytics, brands can gain a deep understanding of their target audiences and tailor their products and campaigns accordingly.

Consumer insights play a crucial role in shaping marketing strategies. These insights provide a window into the needs, desires, and pain points of consumers in different regions. By analyzing this data, brands can identify trends and opportunities that can inform their marketing decisions. For example, understanding the cultural significance of certain holidays or events can help brands create campaigns that resonate with local audiences.

Ethical considerations are also an important aspect of market research.

Brands must ensure that their research practices respect consumer privacy and comply with local regulations. This includes obtaining informed consent from participants and safeguarding their data. By prioritizing ethical research practices, brands can build trust with their consumers and maintain their reputation.

4

Chapter 4: Crafting a Compelling Brand Story

A powerful brand story has the ability to captivate consumers and create emotional connections that transcend cultural boundaries. This chapter explores the elements of a compelling brand narrative and offers guidance on how to adapt your brand story for different cultural contexts.

At the heart of every successful brand story is a clear and authentic narrative that communicates the brand's values, mission, and vision. This narrative serves as a foundation for all marketing efforts and helps to differentiate the brand in a crowded marketplace. In a transnational context, crafting a brand story that resonates with diverse audiences requires a deep understanding of cultural nuances and consumer preferences.

Storytelling is a powerful tool for brand positioning and differentiation. By weaving a narrative that highlights the unique attributes of the brand, marketers can create a memorable and compelling story that stands out in the minds of consumers. This chapter provides examples of successful brand stories and offers practical tips for creating a narrative that resonates with global audiences.

Adapting your brand story for different cultural contexts is essential for building meaningful connections with consumers. This involves understanding the cultural values and traditions that influence consumer behavior and tailoring your narrative to align with these factors. By doing so, brands can create a story that feels authentic and relevant to their target audiences.

5

Chapter 5: Leveraging Digital Marketing Channels

In the digital age, marketing channels are constantly evolving, and brands must stay ahead of the curve to remain competitive. This chapter covers the most effective digital marketing channels for transnational brands and provides strategies for leveraging these channels to reach a global audience.

Social media is one of the most powerful tools for transnational marketing. Platforms like Facebook, Instagram, and Twitter offer brands the opportunity to engage with consumers in real-time and build a global community. By creating culturally relevant content and leveraging the power of social media influencers, brands can amplify their reach and connect with diverse audiences.

Search engine marketing (SEM) is another critical component of digital marketing. By optimizing their websites for search engines and running targeted ad campaigns, brands can increase their visibility and attract potential customers from different regions. This chapter provides tips for effective SEM strategies and highlights the importance of understanding regional search behaviors.

Content marketing is a valuable strategy for building brand awareness and establishing thought leadership. By creating high-quality, culturally relevant content, brands can provide value to their audiences and position themselves as experts in their field. This chapter offers guidance on developing a content marketing strategy that resonates with global audiences and drives engagement.

Adapting digital marketing strategies for different regions and cultural contexts is essential for success. This involves understanding the unique characteristics of each market and tailoring your approach to meet the specific needs and preferences of your target audiences. By doing so, brands can create more effective and impactful digital marketing campaigns.

6

Chapter 6: The Role of Influencer Marketing

In today's digital landscape, influencer marketing has emerged as a powerful tool for brands looking to expand their reach and build credibility. This chapter explores the role of influencers in transnational marketing and provides strategies for identifying and collaborating with the right influencers for your brand.

Influencer marketing involves partnering with individuals who have a significant following on social media or other digital platforms. These influencers can help brands connect with their target audiences in a more authentic and engaging way. By leveraging the influence of local and global influencers, brands can build trust and authenticity with their audiences and effectively communicate their message across different cultural contexts.

Identifying the right influencers for your brand is crucial for the success of your marketing campaigns. This involves researching and evaluating potential influencers based on their audience demographics, engagement rates, and alignment with your brand values. By partnering with influencers who resonate with your target audience, you can create more impactful and meaningful marketing campaigns.

Collaboration is a key aspect of influencer marketing. This chapter provides tips for building strong relationships with influencers, including clear communication, mutual respect, and fair compensation. By fostering positive relationships with influencers, brands can create long-term partnerships that benefit both parties. The chapter also covers the challenges and opportunities of influencer marketing in different cultural contexts and offers strategies for navigating these complexities.

7

Chapter 7: Navigating Legal and Regulatory Challenges

Operating in a global marketplace comes with a host of legal and regulatory challenges. This chapter covers the key legal considerations for transnational brands, including intellectual property rights, data privacy regulations, and advertising standards.

Intellectual property (IP) rights are crucial for protecting your brand's assets, such as trademarks, logos, and product designs. In a transnational context, it is essential to understand the IP laws and regulations in different regions to ensure your brand's assets are adequately protected. This chapter provides guidance on navigating the complexities of IP rights and offers strategies for preventing and addressing IP infringements.

Data privacy regulations are another critical consideration for transnational brands. With the rise of digital marketing, brands must comply with data privacy laws, such as the General Data Protection Regulation (GDPR) in Europe. This involves implementing robust data protection measures and obtaining explicit consent from consumers before collecting and processing their data. By prioritizing data privacy, brands can build trust with their consumers and avoid legal repercussions.

Advertising standards vary across different regions, and brands must ensure their marketing campaigns comply with local regulations. This includes adhering to guidelines on advertising content, disclosure requirements, and marketing practices. By understanding and navigating these challenges, brands can protect their reputation and ensure compliance with local laws. The chapter also discusses the importance of working with legal experts to develop a comprehensive compliance strategy.

8

Chapter 8: Effective Cross-Cultural Communication

Communication is key to building strong relationships with consumers and partners in different regions. This chapter explores the principles of effective cross-cultural communication and provides strategies for adapting your messaging for diverse audiences.

Effective cross-cultural communication involves understanding the nuances of language, tone, and cultural context. By tailoring your messaging to align with the cultural values and expectations of your target audiences, you can create marketing campaigns that resonate with consumers worldwide. This chapter offers practical tips for crafting culturally relevant messaging and avoiding common communication pitfalls.

Cultural sensitivity is an essential aspect of cross-cultural communication. Brands must be aware of cultural differences and avoid stereotypes or offensive content. By conducting thorough research and seeking input from local experts, brands can ensure their messaging is respectful and inclusive. This chapter provides examples of successful cross-cultural communication strategies and highlights the importance of cultural sensitivity in building trust and credibility with global audiences.

In addition to verbal communication, non-verbal communication plays a significant role in cross-cultural interactions. This includes body language, gestures, and visual elements. By understanding the cultural significance of non-verbal cues, brands can create more impactful and meaningful communication strategies. The chapter also covers the role of technology in facilitating cross-cultural communication and offers tips for leveraging digital tools to enhance your marketing efforts.

9

Chapter 9: Localizing Your Marketing Campaigns

Localization is essential for creating marketing campaigns that resonate with local audiences. This chapter covers the process of localizing your marketing campaigns, including adapting your messaging, visuals, and promotional strategies for different regions.

Localization involves more than just translating your content into different languages. It requires a deep understanding of the cultural, linguistic, and market differences that influence consumer behavior. By adapting your messaging and visuals to align with local preferences and expectations, you can create campaigns that feel authentic and relevant to your target audiences.

This chapter provides practical tips for effective localization, including working with local experts, conducting thorough market research, and testing your campaigns with focus groups. By leveraging local insights and expertise, brands can ensure their campaigns are culturally relevant and resonate with their audiences.

Visual elements play a crucial role in localization. This includes adapting your logo, color schemes, and imagery to align with local cultural norms and aesthetics. By creating visually appealing and culturally relevant content, brands can enhance their marketing efforts and build stronger connections with their audiences. The chapter also covers the challenges and opportunities of localization and offers strategies for overcoming common obstacles.

10

Chapter 10: Building Strong Partnerships

Strategic partnerships are a cornerstone of successful transnational marketing. They enable brands to expand their reach, leverage local expertise, and navigate the complexities of new markets. This chapter explores the importance of building strong partnerships with local businesses, distributors, and influencers, and offers strategies for selecting and managing these relationships.

Effective partnerships are built on mutual trust, respect, and shared goals. By collaborating with local partners who have a deep understanding of the market, brands can gain valuable insights and access resources that would otherwise be unavailable. This chapter provides guidance on identifying potential partners, evaluating their capabilities, and establishing clear expectations and communication channels.

Distributors and local businesses play a crucial role in the supply chain and distribution network of transnational brands. By forming strategic alliances with these entities, brands can ensure their products are available and accessible to consumers in different regions. This chapter covers the key considerations for selecting and managing distribution partners, including contractual agreements, performance metrics, and conflict resolution.

Influencers and local opinion leaders can also be valuable partners for transnational brands. By leveraging their credibility and reach, brands can amplify their message and build trust with their target audiences. This chapter offers tips for identifying and collaborating with influencers, including setting clear objectives, providing support and resources, and fostering long-term relationships.

11

Chapter 11: Measuring Success and ROI

Measuring the success of your marketing campaigns is crucial for optimizing your strategies and achieving your goals. This chapter covers the key metrics and tools for measuring the return on investment (ROI) of your transnational marketing efforts.

Data-driven decision-making is essential for effective marketing. By tracking and analyzing key performance indicators (KPIs), brands can gain insights into the effectiveness of their campaigns and make informed decisions. This chapter provides an overview of the most important KPIs for transnational marketing, including brand awareness, engagement, conversion rates, and customer satisfaction.

Marketing analytics tools play a vital role in measuring and evaluating the success of your campaigns. From web analytics platforms like Google Analytics to social media monitoring tools, there are various resources available to help brands track their performance. This chapter offers guidance on selecting the right tools for your needs and leveraging them to gain actionable insights.

Setting clear objectives and benchmarks is essential for measuring success. By defining specific, measurable, achievable, relevant, and time-bound (SMART) goals, brands can track their progress and evaluate the impact of their marketing efforts. This chapter provides tips for setting SMART goals and aligning them with your overall marketing strategy.

Continuous improvement is a key principle of successful marketing. By regularly reviewing and analyzing your performance data, you can identify areas for improvement and refine your strategies. This chapter emphasizes the importance of a feedback loop and offers strategies for using data to drive continuous improvement in your transnational marketing efforts.

12

Chapter 12: Adapting to Changing Market Trends

The global marketplace is constantly evolving, and brands must be agile and adaptable to stay ahead. This chapter covers the importance of staying informed about changing market trends and consumer behaviors, and provides strategies for adapting your marketing strategies accordingly.

Monitoring market trends is essential for identifying new opportunities and anticipating shifts in consumer behavior. This chapter explores the various methods for tracking market trends, including market research, competitor analysis, and social listening. By staying informed about the latest developments in your industry, you can make proactive decisions and stay ahead of the competition.

Consumer behavior is influenced by a range of factors, including cultural, economic, and technological changes. By understanding these influences and how they impact your target audience, you can tailor your marketing strategies to meet their evolving needs. This chapter provides insights into the key drivers of consumer behavior and offers strategies for staying in tune with your audience.

Innovation and creativity are critical for adapting to changing market trends. Brands that embrace new ideas and technologies can differentiate themselves and create unique value propositions. This chapter explores the role of innovation in transnational marketing and offers tips for fostering a culture of creativity within your organization.

Agility and flexibility are essential for responding to market changes. This chapter emphasizes the importance of an agile marketing approach, which involves continuous testing, learning, and iteration. By adopting agile practices, brands can quickly adapt to new trends and opportunities, and maintain a competitive edge in the global marketplace.

13

Chapter 13: Embracing Sustainability and Social Responsibility

Consumers are increasingly demanding that brands act responsibly and sustainably. This chapter explores the importance of integrating sustainability and social responsibility into your transnational marketing strategies.

Sustainability involves adopting practices that minimize environmental impact and promote long-term ecological balance. Brands that prioritize sustainability can build trust and loyalty with their consumers, and differentiate themselves in the marketplace. This chapter provides guidance on implementing sustainable practices in your supply chain, production processes, and marketing campaigns.

Social responsibility goes beyond environmental sustainability to include ethical practices and community engagement. Brands that demonstrate a commitment to social responsibility can enhance their reputation and build stronger connections with their consumers. This chapter explores the various aspects of social responsibility, including fair labor practices, ethical sourcing, and community initiatives.

Promoting sustainability and social responsibility requires transparent and authentic communication. This chapter offers tips for effectively communicating your brand's commitment to sustainability and social responsibility, including leveraging storytelling, certifications, and partnerships with reputable organizations. By being transparent about your efforts and progress, you can build credibility and trust with your audience.

The challenges and opportunities of promoting sustainability in different cultural contexts are also discussed in this chapter. By understanding the local environmental and social issues, brands can tailor their sustainability initiatives to address the specific needs and concerns of their target audiences. This chapter provides strategies for overcoming common obstacles and maximizing the impact of your sustainability efforts.

14

Chapter 14: Navigating Crises and Challenges

Every brand will inevitably face challenges and crises at some point in its journey. How a brand navigates these situations can significantly impact its reputation and long-term success. This chapter covers the key strategies for navigating crises in a transnational context, including crisis communication, reputation management, and damage control.

Crisis communication is the cornerstone of effective crisis management. When a crisis occurs, brands must respond swiftly and transparently to address the concerns of their stakeholders. This chapter provides guidance on developing a crisis communication plan, including identifying key spokespersons, establishing communication channels, and crafting clear and consistent messages. By being prepared and proactive, brands can mitigate the impact of crises and maintain trust with their audiences.

Reputation management is another critical aspect of navigating crises. Brands must work to protect and restore their reputation by taking responsibility, demonstrating empathy, and outlining corrective actions. This chapter explores the strategies for managing reputation during and after a crisis, including monitoring public sentiment, engaging with stakeholders, and leveraging positive media coverage. By showing genuine commitment to resolving the issue, brands can rebuild trust and credibility.

Damage control involves taking immediate actions to address the root cause of the crisis and prevent further harm. This chapter provides tips for effective damage control, including identifying and rectifying the problem, implementing corrective measures, and communicating transparently with affected parties. By taking decisive actions, brands can minimize the negative impact of the crisis and demonstrate their commitment to accountability and improvement.

Learning from challenges is essential for long-term success. This chapter emphasizes the importance of conducting a post-crisis analysis to identify lessons learned and opportunities for improvement. By reflecting on the crisis and implementing changes to prevent future occurrences, brands can strengthen their resilience and build a more robust crisis management strategy.

15

Chapter 15: The Future of Transnational Marketing

The world of transnational marketing is constantly evolving, and brands must be prepared for the future. This chapter explores the emerging trends and technologies that will shape the future of transnational marketing and offers strategies for staying ahead of the curve.

One of the key trends shaping the future of transnational marketing is the rise of artificial intelligence (AI) and machine learning. These technologies are revolutionizing the way brands analyze data, personalize marketing campaigns, and engage with consumers. This chapter provides insights into how AI and machine learning can be leveraged to enhance marketing strategies, improve customer experiences, and drive business growth.

Another emerging trend is the increasing importance of sustainability and social responsibility. As consumers become more conscious of environmental and social issues, brands must prioritize sustainability in their marketing strategies. This chapter explores the opportunities for brands to lead the way in sustainability, from eco-friendly product development to socially responsible marketing campaigns. By embracing sustainability, brands can build stronger connections with their consumers and drive positive change.

The future of transnational marketing also involves greater integration of digital and traditional marketing channels. Brands must adopt an omnichannel approach that seamlessly integrates online and offline experiences. This chapter offers strategies for creating cohesive and integrated marketing campaigns that engage consumers across multiple touchpoints. By providing a consistent and personalized experience, brands can build stronger relationships with their audiences.

Continuous learning and adaptation are essential for staying ahead in the dynamic landscape of transnational marketing. This chapter emphasizes the importance of staying informed about industry trends, seeking out new knowledge, and being open to experimentation. By fostering a culture of innovation and agility, brands can remain competitive and thrive in the global marketplace.

"The Transnational Brand Equation: Crafting Irresistible Global Marketing Strategies":

In today's dynamic global marketplace, businesses must navigate a complex web of cultural nuances, consumer behaviors, and market trends to succeed. "The Transnational Brand Equation: Crafting Irresistible Global Marketing Strategies" is your ultimate guide to mastering the art of transnational marketing and building a brand that resonates with audiences around the world.

This comprehensive book takes you on a journey through the essential principles and strategies for creating a powerful global brand identity. From understanding the intricacies of diverse markets to leveraging the latest digital marketing channels, you'll gain valuable insights and practical tips for crafting marketing campaigns that captivate and engage consumers across different cultural contexts.

Through real-world examples and case studies, "The Transnational Brand Equation" explores the role of cultural intelligence, effective communication, and strategic partnerships in driving global marketing success. You'll learn how to build strong relationships with local influencers, navigate legal and regulatory challenges, and measure the impact of your marketing efforts.

The book also delves into the importance of sustainability and social responsibility in today's consumer landscape, offering strategies for integrating

CHAPTER 15: THE FUTURE OF TRANSNATIONAL MARKETING

ethical practices into your marketing campaigns. With a forward-looking perspective on emerging trends and technologies, you'll be equipped with the knowledge and tools to stay ahead in the ever-evolving world of transnational marketing.

Whether you're a seasoned marketer or a business leader looking to expand your brand's global reach, "The Transnational Brand Equation: Crafting Irresistible Global Marketing Strategies" provides the insights and strategies you need to thrive in the international marketplace. Discover how to create a brand that transcends borders and captivates the hearts and minds of consumers worldwide.

www.ingramcontent.com/pod-product-compliance
Lightning Source LLC
LaVergne TN
LVHW020740090526
838202LV00057BA/6136